Playtime

Poems & Art

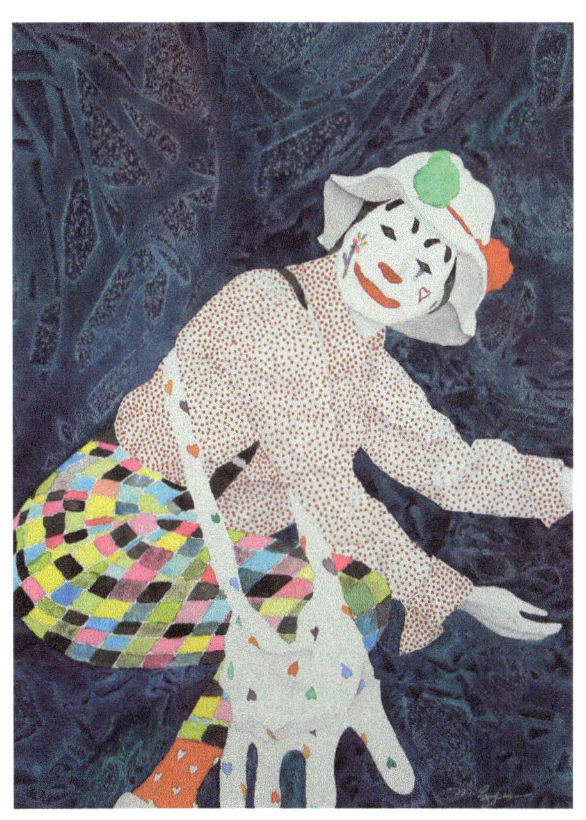

Mary Eggers

Cover painting, "It's About Love," watercolor by Mary Eggers
Cover Design: Mary Eggers
Editor: Frank Simons
Book Design: Mary M Meade
Authors photo: Tom Roberts

First Edition:
ISBN 978-1-969122-06-4

This Book is Lovingly Dedicated
to
Lois Read

A dear friend, talented artist,
and gifted poet.

Thank you for introducing me to
San Miguel de Allende,
poet Judyth Hill,
and the love of my life,
Frank Simons.

CONTENTS

II. Speaking Out

III. Love

Preface

As I've worked on this, my second book of poetry, in the fall of 2025, I've been more aware than ever before of the need for speaking out, and for love. Speaking out, not in anger or to harm, rather to engage and understand. And love, as my poem "Yes" says, "everywhere I look—Love," between two people or the sunlight and rain the joys and pains of life." I want to love them all. And finally, there's the section titled Playing with Words. I believe it's important to find time to play, for me it is with paint and poetry—what is it for you?

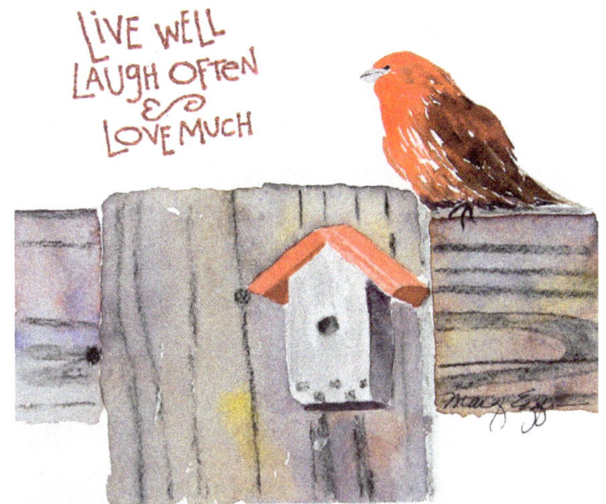

"Nope—Too Small," Watercolor, 6"x6"

1. Playing With Words

Dancing Cobblestones

Pick a street any street
in San Miguel de Allende
today Clavel has been
chosen.

So begins the dance of the
cobblestones … they take them up
do the hokey pokey turn them around
and put them back down.

Now my large family of stones
looks just the same … except
they have new dance partners
that they don't know.

The b…e...a…t of the hammers are silent
while the dance floor is vacant
still uneven … and just like before
too dangerous to dance on.

Cats Cavorting Crazily

Abbie acts asinine
BW bounce from black to white
Charlie chases chickens
Darky darts into dark doorways
Echo eats everything
Fluffy flirts fiercely
George gets jealous
Happy hunts hairballs
Indie investigates envelops
Jumpy jumps jubilantly
Kitty kisses cumquats
Linus licks loving lips
Merlin makes magic
Ninny naps with Vinny
Oscar opens ovens
Pussy purrs perfectly
Queenie quiets quickly
Rascal runs riotously
Sugar sits serene
Tiger trips tenderly
Ursi uses umbrellas
Violet vexes virtuously
Wilson whine whimsically
X x-rays x-mas
YaYa yawns with yellow
Zorro zips Zs

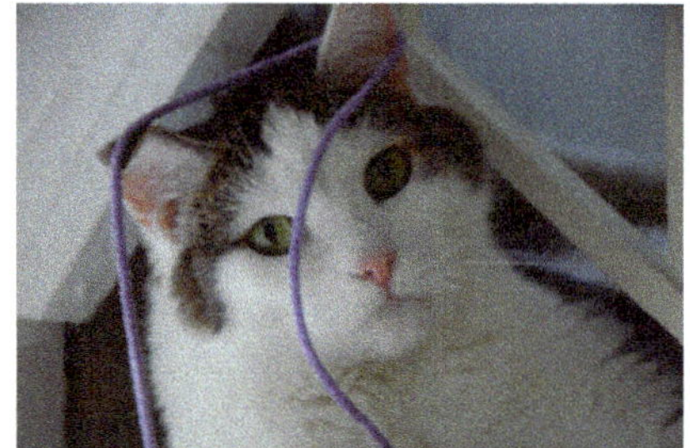

Merlin

Loose

A side-show mystery
becomes the main event
in the main tent
a fact that is
futile to ignore.

On this mysteriously beautiful
day with stars, moon and sun
all glowing at once while every
shadow glistens with fairy dust
why would anyone
want to ignore anything?

Poppy a clown at six
is the main event
in the main tent
she can cause you
to laugh or cry … to hold on tight or
go delightfully loose.

Every movement she makes is
delightfully loose …
because clowns
are always loose
tightness just doesn't go
with laughter and silliness.

You could choose victory over tightness
by joining the mystery of the side-show
and becoming delightfully loose.

Delicious

Hours in a silent garden with a
    delicious naughty novel
        losing all sense of time and place
no one around yet called to look up … to see
    a delicious smear of luminous
        orange with a whisper of pink
across a blue sky.

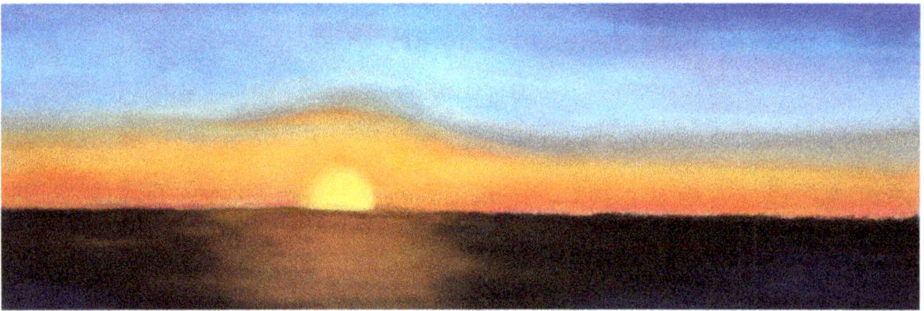

"His Sunset," pastel, 7"x20"

A Poet's Window

It's 3am with an emptiness
that speaks of silence—speaking
without sound.

A man in a pink hoodie
walks up the street in silence
the red bucket marks a reserved
parking space in silence.

To add to the silence
tall Tuscan evergreen stand
without moving telling me
there is no wind.

All while the paper boats
float without sound through the
mural on the wall across the street.

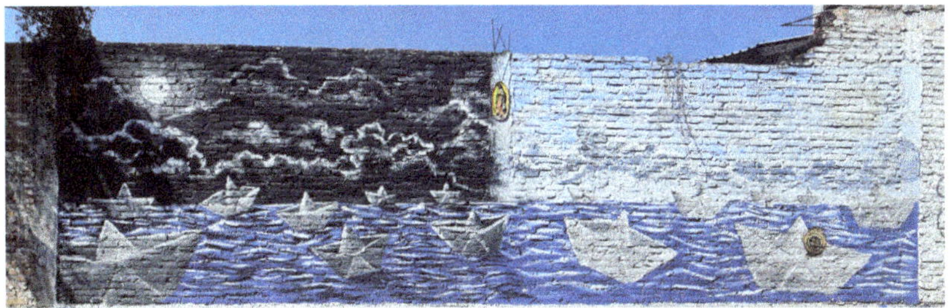

Paper Boats Mural, photo by Mary Eggers

I Want Playtime

Words they escape me
where are the ones that rhyme
tell me your story—sit on my knee
I want you to face me and shine.

Open me—fill me with glee
I'll buy you for pennies or give you a dime
don't ignore me or let me be
help this poet to rhyme.

A Wicked Bed

Was the wicked witch
    all bad?
She wore black that she
    looked really good in.
Creative she was
    full of life, love, joy
        and mystery.

She slept in a wicked bed
    so some said - because
they heard strange sounds
    from the room and
sometime found shoes that
    were not hers outside her door.

Passion In the Park

I arrive to feathery shades of green
from a Hummingbird tree lit by the sun
to create shade for blending their white magic embrace
before becoming beauty in flight.
Stairs held in a profusion
of fuchsia bougainvillea
while rags hang from a limb
and the park wall gets dressed up
with a fresh new coat of orange.

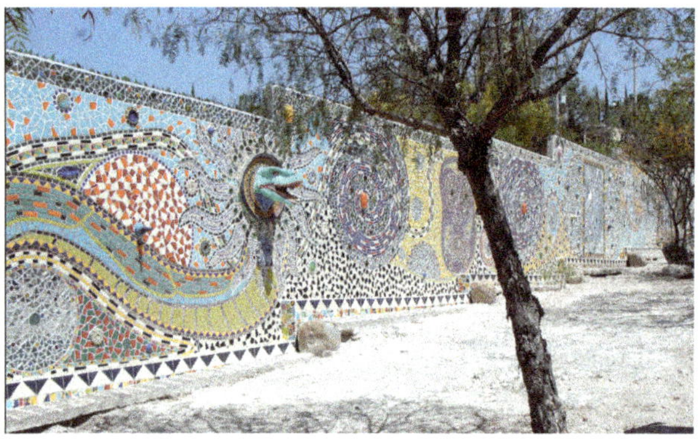

The Chapel of Jimmy Ray

At the End of the Hill

I've a tiny back yard with a huge playground near … all mine …
well … not all mine

At the playground on any given day you might find:
three ducks standing on water,
a heron and turtle gazing at each other while resting on a log,
a lake that is endangered because of neglect,
blue sky with cirrus or cumulus clouds shaped
like us kissing,
a background forest of oak, walnut and beech,
fishing poles in the hands of young boys,
a new bridge that wasn't needed,
and the eagles that live here.

Into the Night

The white hot
    light
through the
    trees
now descends some …
goes lower
behind a dark
patch of leaves.

In a moment
it will fall into the next
    opening
and then a moment later
disappear into
    the night.

Dogwood II

Each day you give a new surprise
today red berries
yesterday the sun
set fire to a few leaves
tomorrow....
tomorrow there will be less green
and more gold.

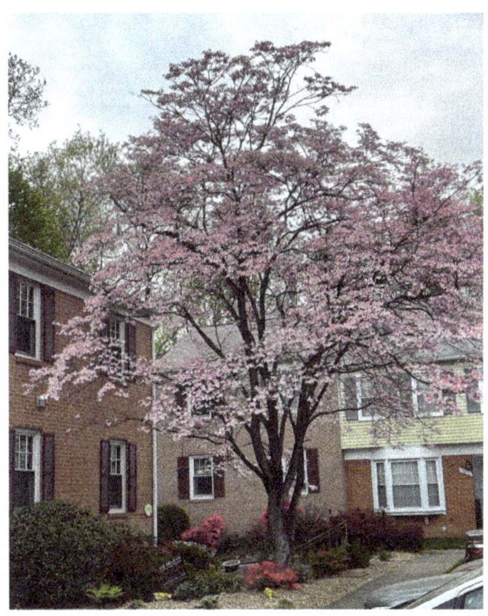

Pink Dogwood

Another Direction

I linger longer
    I'm captured by a bird's eye view
        of the folds of a white sheet.

        Folds have led to unfolding's
    some new direction in my life ...
these folds are different
    they're here—now—holding me
        in their beauty.

        Soft grays turning to almost black,
    then bleeding into bold white
as light comes through.
    A sensuous curve of
        one shape --- takes me
in another direction.
    Releasing me to see
        with eyes shut
            what is beyond seeing.

The Path Not Taken

While listening to Jazz
an adventure begins
at an art festival pizzazz.
Two dear friends … *gold dust twins*
intelligent and creative
lose their car.

Yes, they lose their car.
They park, walk, talk
and lose themselves in art.
Paintings from scraps of cloth
others covered in bees wax
and oh so much beautiful glass.

Full of their own creative ideas
they walk to the car … that's not there.
Great exercise they're getting
grateful for the day.
Passing landmarks on the way
yet … no car.

Retracing their steps many times
doesn't help.
The police say "not towed,"
a loved one gives encouragement.
Now they take the path not taken
and there she sits.

An Artist's Story

This is no nursery rhyme
it's a true story.
It sparkles with color
rainbows of them
Jazz music too and exhibits
from New York to California.

There were watercolor sketches
from her travels, and of course
paintings in her studio.

There were solo exhibits
"The Unfolding" her first
so titled for the unfolding of her life,
paintings of the people
of Bhutan, India, and Nepal.

A photograph of the single curl
of a boat's bow wave on the
Chesapeake Bay
entered and awarded.

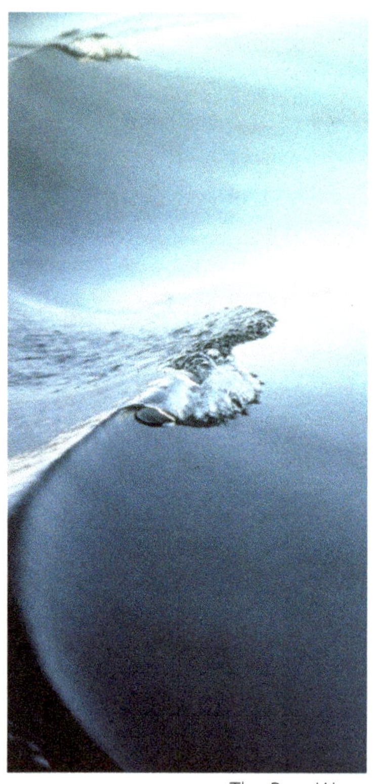
The Bow Wave

Soon to be at the Art League Gallery
her love of Jazz and painting
come together with
paintings of Jazz musicians
a solo exhibit titled
"And All That Jazzz."

A Dance with Lois and BC

I fall asleep right away
thanks to the wine
at 2:30am I'm awake
thanks to wine.

I turn to my usual remedy, yummy
hot chocolate and poetry by Lois
Read or Billy Collins. This time,
as with others when I'm ready

I return to bed hearing their rhythm and rhyme
as they chime "write" and a new poem
inspired by Lois and BC
slow dances me to sleep.

The Rope

My grandparents
I'm across the street
from the house they lived in …
when a little old lady that looks
a bit like my grandmother turns
goes up the concrete steps
walks the path to the wooden steps
to the front door and goes in
    … while I wonder.

Now all these years later what
does the house look like inside, do I dare?
Yes, as I once again walk up the concrete steps
the path to the wooden steps
and knock on the door.

She answers, I share my history with the house.
She invites me in. All I see is a memory
my grandfather on a single bed under the steps
leading to the second floor.
A rope hangs from the banister above—
the rope gives him freedom.
I once again see him lift himself in and out
of bed and wheelchair… without help.
He is good … kind … funny and he loves me a lot.

Returning to the present moment, I'm stunned …
I see her husband sitting on the bed
under the stairs his wheelchair next to him …
like my grandfather he has no legs below the knee.
    A rope hangs from the banister above.

This Moment

It took a fraction of a moment
to lose myself … all of myself
over the loss of one *thing*

craziness overtook
stopped my breath
raced my heart
filled me with fear
all for one *thing*

how—how did this happen
in an instant I was gone
as I forgot what is real

now in a moment of stillness
I am free to hold this
sacred moment
and this sacred moment
and this sacred moment
for this sacred moment
is all that is real.

Life in San Miguel de Allende, I

Washed clean
a favorite bright pink top
hanging free
on a clothesline.
The wind picked up
now it hangs free
40 feet above the street
on a utility line,
while I puzzle how.
The wind picked up
dropped it on
the street below
at my feet.

Bump in the Road

I find myself about to step
    yet uncertain about
stepping. I am uniquely qualified
    to guide a long standing
gem of a poetry group over
    a bump in the road … and?

Why, I'm asking has this landed
    so firmly in my awareness?
Helping our poetry group run smoother
    why can't I let it go, let the
chips land where they may? Am I
    making too much of this?

Yes, of course Lois was the right
    person to listen.
We talked about her letting go
    and my building …
a love, a life, a community.
    That's why I'm going to
step in and offer my best.

Chosen

I get an e-mail business inquiry and reply
without noticing who or where it's from,
they want a draft proposal, that's an easy "yes."
We discuss specifics like timeframe
outcomes, number of people and that
I'll ask one of my partners to join me.

After a break I go back to the e-mail
to find that my client, Susan, works for Airbus…
you know the ones that make very
big airplanes. She's is at their headquarters
in Toulouse in the south of France, I dream
of going a week early to enjoy the city.

They have chosen to bring *me* to Toulouse
France and pay *me* for being there. I'm
too excited about Toulouse to think
about the work now, except for asking
my partner Paul to join me … he lives in Austria
which will make expenses less for Airbus.

The flight and train are long and although
I should be tired I'm out for a walk.
Toulouse in September where the streets
are full of folks enjoying the fall weather,
no I don't speak French though
I fall in love with everyone that does.

I have a week of holiday before work starts.
Toulouse a city I can get lost and found in
I walk exploring every nook and cranny

finding a carousel in the center of town,
I take a spin just like the other kids
smiling the whole way round.

I'm going to splurge … enjoy French wine
foods, pastries and the art around every corner.
The art of buildings, ceilings, street musicians,
clowns with red noses even a plaza where
couples dance the sexiest of all dances—tango.
I enjoy a second glass before my walk home.

I'm half way through my week of holiday,
when I decide to rent a car—it speaks English
is programmed to get me to my destination,
St Cirq Lapopie, high up on a cliff overlooking
the river. In this little village I find "Mary Peinter"
a gallery named for me … can this be?

Count Down

Three days and counting   I am not a wimp
    I am
        rugged!
Experimenting over the days to come
    with just how rugged.

Today was to be a blues festival
    instead it's preparation
Tomorrow, Sunday … a day of rest yet … not this Sunday.

Time before filled with things I won't
    be able to do after for a while …
workout at the gym
    walk around my lake
        yoga
            walking will be slow
stairs even slower   can't drive for a time.

Remember—I am rugged
    will take it all in stride
        will close my eyes and lay silent
            meditation bench is out for now.

It's not a three day count down
    it's until this rugged young woman
        is dancing with joy.

My Problem with Poetry

A page from Billy Collins ....
I don't have a hankering for words
I can't pronounce—and those are many.
A remnant of being dyslexic,
which I am slightly, its enough
to cause me problems when
reading someone else's poetry.
I long for simple easy words,
that roll off my tongue like honey
oozing out of the honeycomb.
Even when I read a word
that's not on the page couldn't
I at least read a simple one?

A Dry Spell

The shadow of a poet
longs for the magical muse
to visit and save her from silence.
It's been a while since she's ventured
into the junkyard of words
where unspoken words wait to be spoken.

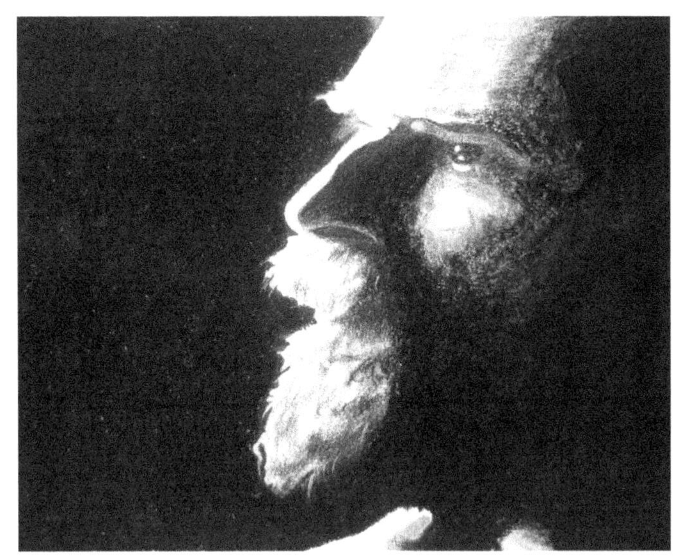

"Out of the Dark," Charcoal 11"x15"

II. Speaking Out

Seven Circles

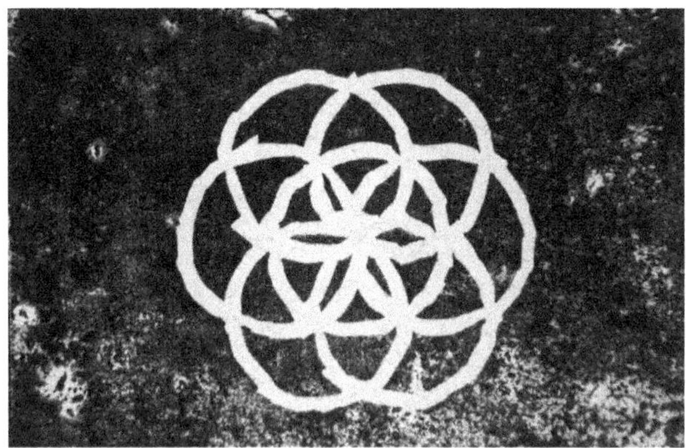

The Earth Flag

They are the earth
of the future.
The one my heart and perhaps
yours long for
and may never
experience.

They hold the promise of acceptance for all.
They have let go of ownership,
borders and fear of difference.

They
Are
The
Earth
Flag.

Our Hypocrisy

Will you ever feel their
    tears … the cries of
the dying — or of
    the ones who remain?

You pray—and nothing changes
    and you still pray
and nothing changes.

YOU—congress, YOU the president
    YOU the governors, mayors,
priests and pastors
    YOU the public—do nothing
except pray
    yet the killing continues.

    In the first 23 days of the new year
        37 mass shootings
            sixty-two dead
                one hundred seventy-one injured.
Will you ever stop praying
    and act?

Control

These Supremes are not the ones of
    the 60s that sang beautifully.
Six of these nine decide to control
    women in the   United States.

Millions of my sisters and I have
    no rights … remember the
ERA for women has no
                    Constitutional weight.

Some women seem not to want rights …
    they like being told what to think.
"Pro-life" now means ending another's right
                    to a safe gate.

Others, like me, wonder …
1973 Roe control granted … wait isn't control
of my body my birth right—it is for men.
2022 the six take it away …   doesn't translate.

Before '73, what if …
    abuse at six or at 16
        me pregnant
a child turned mother …   can't relate.

Six eliminate a woman's right to choose
    politics and power … now control
        my body …
                    my fate.

While "...life, liberty and pursuit of happiness..."
are just words on a page ...
without weight.

Earth Day 2023

A long time fascination
with this wild cat
first turned into an art sculpture
in China in 5000 BC.

The largest of the big cats … they are strong,
beautiful, independent with shrew perception
warm-hearted yet fearsome,
courageous when facing danger
yet yielding, soft and mysterious.

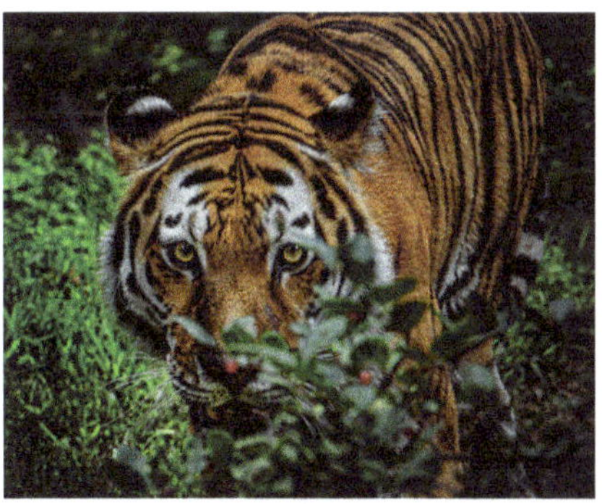

In many cultures they are a symbol of the
sacred union of feminine and Mother Earth
and considered a guardian deity.
They are now captured in the deadly
grip of human misuse.

Tigers are vanishing
for the children of tomorrow
will they find the wild things
fascinating when seen only in photographs?

Difference

Two, one tall, thin
    and smooth,

the other taller
    bigger
        rough.

Close
    touching
all the way up.

Roots growing over roots

two different trees
standing together
growing together.

Why can't we?

Windows of Color

What do you choose … to see?
Only black and white …
do you even allow your eyes to see
the infinite creativity in human form?
There are the primaries red blue and yellow
from these with a little black or white
    every other color comes.

What about the shades of brown
that are found in all of us
the glow of iridescent copper, burnt sienna
brown ocher, raw sienna, indian red
we all are some shade of these.
And now the rainbow colors
that speak to us with Pride
    we are all just human beings.

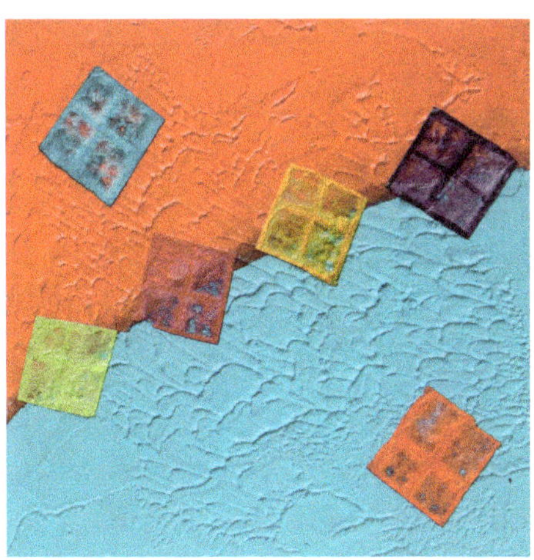

"Windows of Color," Acrylic, 8"x8"

Who Loses?

Banned book
    banned abortion
        more guns
            fewer school days.

Books banned … so say conservative
school districts.
    273 books in 2020,
        377 in 2019
            483 in 2018 …
another of our rights dwindling.

Banned abortion—so says the high court
    women no longer have
        control of their body.

More guns—so says the high court
    398 million owned now
20 million of them assault rifles
    another 250 million high capacity magazines.
US population in 2020—329 million …
    you do the math. Will we be safer—not likely.

In Texas the teacher shortage is addressed by
    shortening the school week by one day
vs. paying teachers a better wage.

Who loses? We all do!

Locked in Locked Out

My country's promise grabs you
fills you with better, safer, more
of everything lacking in your country.
It's promise fills your heart and mind
locks out every other message.

Never real this promise … not for you
with black, brown or olive skin,
eyes that slant, a voice that speaks
of a lesser country … we have forgotten
the US was founded by immigrants.

My country's promise has locked you in
my whiteness has locked you out.
Locked out of better, safer, more.
You are an immigrant … legal or not
    a spick
        a chink
            an illegal alien
                an outsider.

As We Look Away

Digested by time and neglect
    we ignored the first
wrinkle on earth's face
    saying "this won't last."

As we look away
    pretending it will go away
on its own.

Digested by time and neglect
    the earth on fire
streets full of fish
    from sea level rise

As we look away
    knowing it won't go away
on its own.

Who Will Rise

If this dark duo should die
who will rise
will they be as evil
and care for none other
than money and power.

Will our better angles survive
to lift us up out of despair
removing the rose colored glasses
allowing all to see the truth of destruction.

November 5, 2024

Democracy—deleted or saved
Exclusion or inclusion
Money over what matters
Oligarchy or enough for everyone
Constitution upheld—maybe not
Rs & Ds working together—what a dream
Authoritarian or humanitarian
Civility verses rudeness
Yes or no to Democracy.

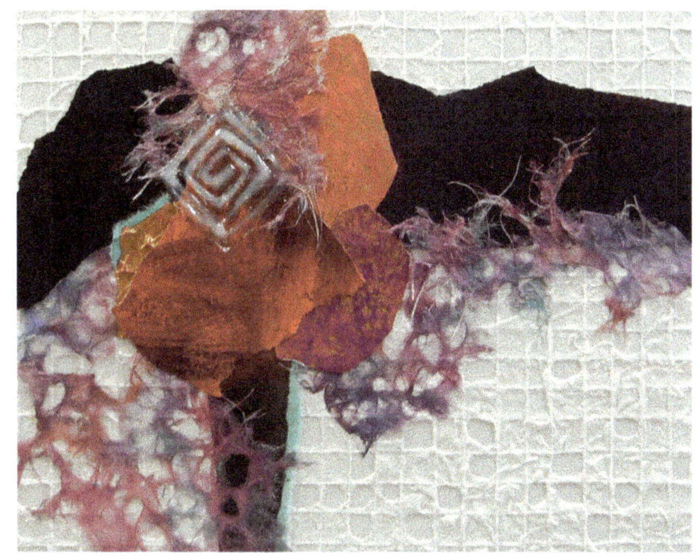

"A Time for Love," Collage, 11"x11"

III. Love

Teach Me

You give me pink and
white in the spring
then you let go.
In the fall it's red, gold
with very little green left
the sun shines through
and illuminates all
then you let go.
Do you feel that … does it hurt?
Will you teach me …
to let go.

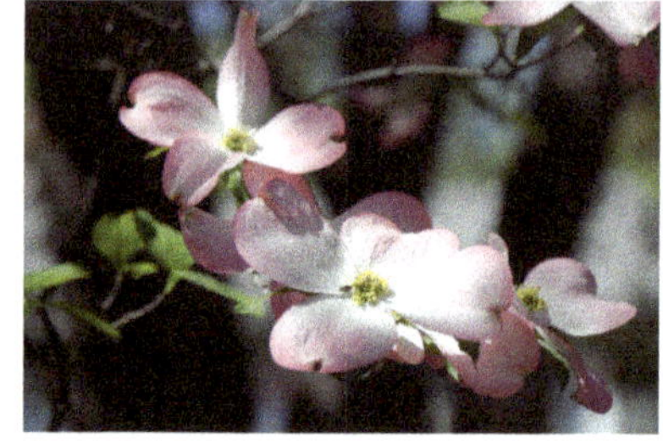

Dogwood Blossoms

The Girl

...And the seasons they go round and round
The girl soon completes her
seventy seventh circle—looking behind
seeing strength, courage and creativity.

There were pains of deaths because she loved
there was a rewarding career because she risked it all
there were deep spiritual leanings because
she said yes when her inner voice spoke.

...And the painted ponies go up and down
Far and wide she traveled to learn about the world
in Uganda the people of Kolongo dance for her,
with a group of friends she went to Bhutan,
India and Nepal returning to create
eighteen paintings of their people.

...We're captive on a carousel of time
In her fortieth circle she started
graduate school—gutsy doing it
without an undergrad ... scared of it all
until a friend's wise advice.

...We can't return, we can only look
She looked here and there in all
the wrong places for love not just
any love that one special love.

...Behind, from where we came
She came from modest beginnings
a difficult family life, depression,

joys, sorrows—in time she learned
to hold on to the joys and let go of the rest.

...And go round and round and round,
in the circle game

Now love's come callin on the wind
...she's opened her heart and let it in.

"Yes!"

What does one do
      …when
they have fallen in love
      with love?
Is there anything else
      to fall in love with?

Everywhere I look—Love:
      the lamp light,
the man next to me on his cell,
the table cloth,
all the voices in this delicious
      Italian restaurant,
where I again will
      fall in love with …
grilled calamari.

This love isn't about a
      he or him,
it's about a life well lived
      an adventure
where I've said
"Yes!" over and over.
Yes to Uganda and Kalongo, Iraqi art,
a moon ritual in Bhutan,
yes to Kathy and meaningful work,
      yes to Shalom and yes again and again!
            yes to death ... rebirth mine,
                  yes to the smile sitting next to me,
                        yes to Calamari Alla Griglia.
      Yes!

Ritz Crackers

In a park at the foot of the
Blue Ridge Mountains, a party
it's summer though not so hot
her oldest all the way from Kansas City
her youngest all the way from Vienna, Virginia
mom the middle of four brothers
my grandmother, dressed in pink,
in the seat of honor on her 90th.

Moving from a large farm house on
a hundred acres, she now
lives alone in a little four-room
house with indoor plumbing—no more
snakes in the outhouse for us, no more
drawing water from the well, she and granddad
farmed their whole life, that's what
grew her strong of stature, will and strength.

Proud of her little house always neat
everything in its place
a root cellar for potatoes, beets,
carrots, turnips—I didn't like turnips!
Now remembering round Ritz Crackers,
the very best buttered toast made
on an old wood stove—my grandmother
like the Blue Ridge sitting well-grounded
and true in her chair rocking.

My Word

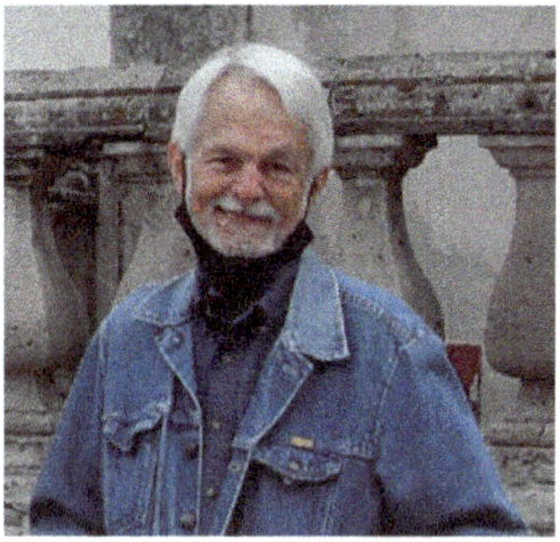
Frank Simons

It could be French like a French kiss
    or the French Franc
it is often direct, open, honest.
Never blunt, bold or brazen
    it's a solid drum beat.

My word is not capricious
    the word is often easy,
uninhibited, truthful and free
never boastful, ambiguous or indirect
    the truth is....

My word isn't just any old word
    it's a heart-to-heart connection
where awe and wonder are rolled into
a place of rest ... a place to be held
    my word is Frank. And...

the French Kisses aren't bad either.

A Spark

I wonder if the hippopotamus
feels the tiger's whiskers
when they kiss?
Are they in love—how odd
they're so different.
He weighs three thousand pounds
she about 300 pounds.
He 16 hours a day in water
and water and cats don't mix.
Yet there's a spark between them,
if we humans paid attention we could learn
something about loving differences.

Blue

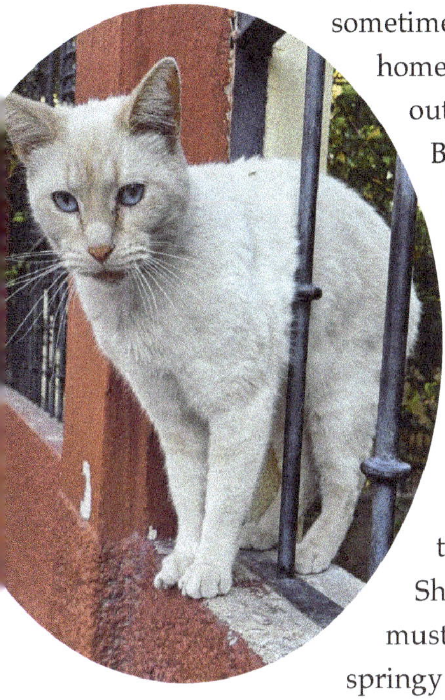

Every day I visit her
sometimes home sometimes not
home being a small garden
outside a building across the street.
Blue—for her siempre azul eyes.
She hears my voice and comes
to the spot where we meet
both rugged from her years alone
and very gentle and trusting.
When we meet she blesses me
with a head bump and sometimes
by putting her paw on my cheek
she opens me to reverence
teaching me about trust.
She is poetry in motion and she
must speak Siamese given her color
springy as she jumps up to the ledge
she is a gata I've learned to love.

Our Singing Poet

Young, tall, really cute with blue eyes
to fall in love with. He *smells peace lilies*
growing in the meadow on a distant breeze.
His slight British accent doesn't show up in his singing.

He sits caressing his guitar, companion
to the soft sung words of his powerful
poems set to music ... his lyrics are strong
his voice is bright he sings like a soft breeze.

I wonder if this special singing poet
knows how easy it is for us
to love him and his poems.

Peace

The gift of art, you know
that feeling
creating something outside
yourself … yet
coming from within you.

Letting everything else drop away
in the moments of creation
color—form—mistakes—successes
you love them all.

It soothes like nothing else.
It slows you—holds you
caresses you in the moment.
Leaves only peace.

Momentum

In the face of it, do I have any control
do I even want control?
Starting slow then like a star shooting across the sky
reaching its destination in a flash.
Going deeper and deeper
while dancing - dancing full out
filled with delight!

This momentum
has a life of its own separate from me
yet it's my life.

It sneaks into the tiny little spaces
cleans them out ...
surprisingly, I'm okay with that.

Things have come and now things are going—just things.
New exciting experiences replacing old things.
Could I stop this ... could I step back and say wait I'm not ready?

I can't say I don't know how, that would be cheating
given what I do know
and time's too precious to cheat.

There isn't an answer so live Rilke suggestion ...
"forget the answers and live the question."

You Were Present

Right next to me … warm touching me
 holding me, you know this place
  its significance in my life
   you wanted me to feel you.

Morning meditation … you honored
 the sacred spot
  where you would sit
   again you were present.

Stones, labyrinth, high meadow
 Judy's arch into the forest … letting go
  new openings trusting my intentions
   you were present.

You held me in the dance this morning
 wrapped your arms around me
  warmed my heart … because
   you were present.

You are the beloved present
 of my life.

Tribute

Chorus
If I said you had a beautiful body would you hold it against me?
If I swore you were an angel would you treat me like the devil tonight?
If I were dying of thirst would your flowing love come quench me?
If I said you had a beautiful body would you hold it against me?

Days of isolation—alone—me and music
knowing we're all in this pan
demic, together?
Sorry the pan's just big enough for one.

Repeat the chorus …

I'm an old hippie and I don't know what to do.
Should I hang on to the old, should I grab onto the new.
I'm not old and I missed being a hippie
looked like fun and not me—then anyway,
now hanging onto the old often seems like a really
good idea.
Grab onto the new—it's all virtual
and you can't grab that, and remember
the pan's just big enough for one
so I can't even grab you.

Repeat the chorus …

So, let that feelin' grab you deep inside
And send you reelin' where your love can't hide
And let your love shine and you'll know what I mean
It's the season.

Any CD that starts with *Let Your Love Flow*
    is my cup of tea
        or maybe my margarita…
it's 5pm somewhere in the world.
No, you can't join me—though it would be
    much more fun if you did…
damn that pan anyway!

Repeat the chorus …

My Friday date, ALL night LONG, with the Bellamy Brothers…
    yes, I'm a two-man woman
        and … proud of it!
Dreams can make anything possible,
    even in this little pan.

Hallelujah
Let me sock it to ya
Praise the Lord and pass the tambourine.

A Premonition

A morning dream titled … 99 Pleasures
    or was it a preview of
        coming attractions?
Can I remember the first
    man that touched me
        or the electricity that ran through me?

Will I ever experience it again
    spooning the deliciousness of being held
        your hand moving slowly … warm … tender
as you say my name … that was the dream.
    Now it's a deep soul's longing coming true
        one day … one step … three words at a time.

Twilight

As the setting sun
kisses my back fence
inviting twilight and coolness
I ready myself for an evening walk
while thinking of love's kisses to come.

Waiting on the Muse

Is it done
    the looking, testing
    one thing then
        another.
Standing back—-do I like it?
    Maybe.
A "yes" can't be pushed
    or demanded.
What then is there to do……..except
    to love the painting process
and wait on the muse.

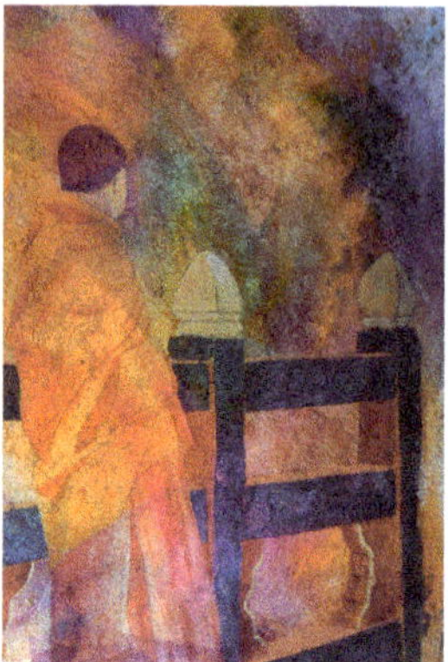

"Dreaming at Para Dzong,"
Acrylic, 14"x10"

Where the Laundry Leads

In the midst of *too much*
that all feels unruly
a project that takes me
back to the past when doing
    this work was easy.

Age or distance and
too much to fit into
    too little time.

So I start the laundry
and there before me
a most beautiful sunset
as earth again shifts
    and night falls.

I stand in awe and wonder
silence in me
    silence in this sunset

Memories

The night window
filled with reflections of a dark wall
a painting of yellow flowers
and a ceiling fan …
ordinary stuff.

Yet these are my memory makers
of cool breezes
the painting's artist
in Ann Arbor
and the installer of the fan.

In the surrounding room
my grandmother
holds a family mostly passed,
while paintings, a ceramic clown
and photographs
create an artistic delight.

All as a glass of red
from a bottle of poetry
gently sends me to sleep.

From Beijing To Hong Kong

As often I do I just start walking without a destination ... sometimes get lost always get found even here in Beijing China. This time I stumble upon a most engaging little gem of a house and the art of Qi Baishi who lived there until his death in 1957.

His house with a center garden is now a museum of his life and art ... I fall head over heals in love with both. His paintings seem like visual poems in their simplicity, elegance and the passion that each piece holds.

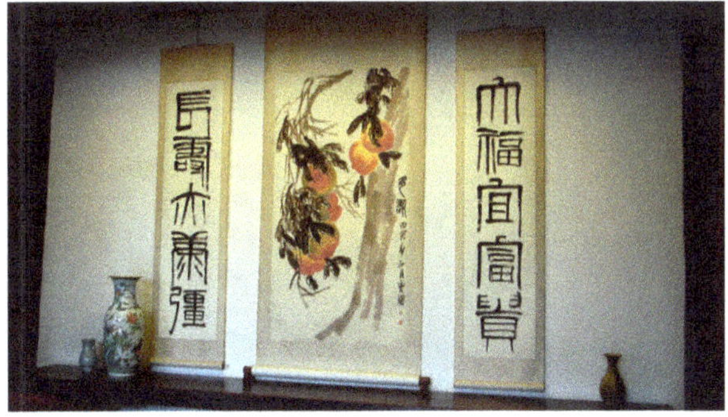

Qi Baishi's Art

Day two and I'm drawn back to his house to just sit in the garden and reflect on what Qi Baishi might have been like when he started painting. He learned his style from the Manual of the Mustard Seed Garden printed in the early Qing Dynasty sometime in the 1600s.

My time in China is filled with surprises like
spending the evening on my own at a jazz club
after figuring how to find my way there and back
using the underground, returning to my hotel room
still hearing my favorite music.

I skip the Pandas … our National Zoo has
them, spend the day with a good friends
daughter who teaches Kendo in Chengdu.
It's a national holiday the city is packed
shoulder to shoulder in some places which
tires me out so it's home to bed early.

My last day is in Hong Kong spent in the art
district wondering in and out … until I see in a
window *Memories Of A Master Qi Baishi,*
My Grandfathers Ink Paintings by Xiong Zhichun.
A perfect gift from one artist to another.

A Christmas Painting

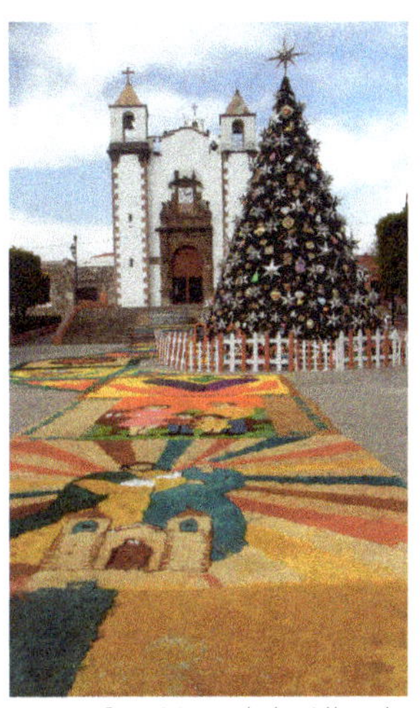
San Miguel de Allende

In Barrio San Antonio in
San Miguel de Allende is the
San Antonio church with steps
leading to an always open door.

Early morning church bells ringing
through the San Antonio neighborhood
both church and a little tienda next door
welcoming everyone who passes.

From the church's open door down the steps
there's a small plaza with manicured trees,
seasonal flowers, benches to rest in the sun,
children playing while dogs are resting.

During this time of year the plaza transforms
a large tree, silver star, balls of color, twinkle lights,
a picket fence around the base—just like dad's picket
fence around my family's tree when I was a child.

A Christmas painting, created with colored sawdust begins at
the top, flows down each step through the plaza to a street,
each section a new design lovingly painted by families from
San Antonio's community, as a tribute to the Christmas birth.

Handmade Quilts

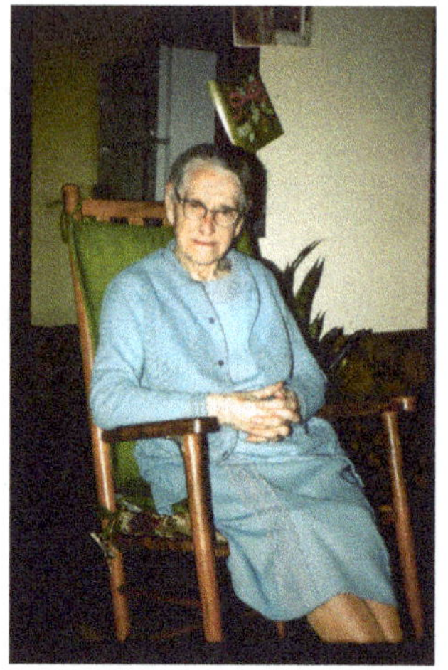
The Quilt Maker

On the way to grandma's house
stopping for Dairy Queen of course.
Arriving at the farmhouse
grandma sitting outside pumping
up - down turning cream into butter.

On bath day, a big metal tub
in the center of the kitchen
water heated on a wood stove.
One didn't linger and the water
wasn't changed after every bath.

I'm youngest so sent to bed first
cold winter nights a dark room upstairs,
under mountains of her handmade quilts
the warmth of the hands that made them
cradled me to sleep and hold me through the night.

The Fuchsia Bougainvillea

Surrounded by the most
vibrant of colors
the sun welcoming my body…
I'm meeting him. Lois would say
"Mr. Right"… is he?
Sally would say "don't over
analyze this"… am I?
With him or thinking of him
I feel delight, and
for now delight feels just right.

The Gift

I'm waiting for the future
to become the present.
Where the present
is a gift extraordinaire!

The gift of an open heart
with open arms
where all paths are inviting.

As music plays day and night
and fireworks sound
whenever they please.

Surrounding ourselves
with color and light
we hold each other with ease.

My Canyons

Not the Grand with its
dry stone walls, rapids, ice cold
water and tent sleeping.
Where I spent a week white water rafting
300 miles of the Colorado River
with my friend Mary Ellen.

This is about Copper Canyon
seen mostly by train weaving through
its 89 mountain tunnels and over 36 bridges.
Where my friend Lois and I spent nights
in colonial inns with one of our
guides playing guitar and singing.

The region, home to the Tarahumara native Mexicans
one of the largest tribes in North America.
They are known for 100 mile barefoot runs
and the most beautiful handmade baskets.
You can buy one at the next train stop.

Lois and I skipped the zip line
in favor of the gondola across the canyon
as we watched those that zipped by.
Stayed a night with a balcony that dropped
off to the mile plus canyon floor below.
Both friends gone now while
memories remain.

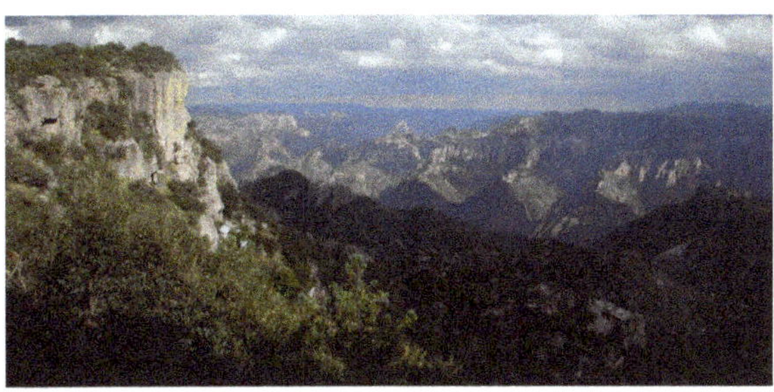

Copper Canyon, Mexico

My Magical Book

Though the house is old now
 it's still a work of art with sixteen rooms
  the moon high and the sun setting in each.

Every room a new focus
 one with cats next to birds
  ...they get along just fine.

There's a room full of jazz
 one of the people of Bhutan
  another of butterflies and penguins.

Abstract art is scattered throughout
 all held together with silver stars.

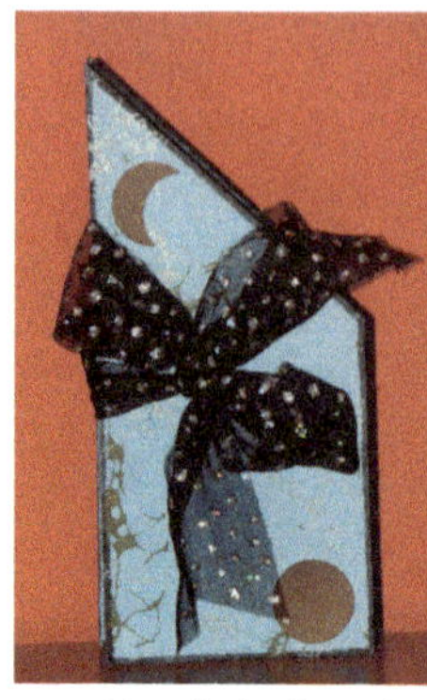

Untitled, 7″x3¼″x1

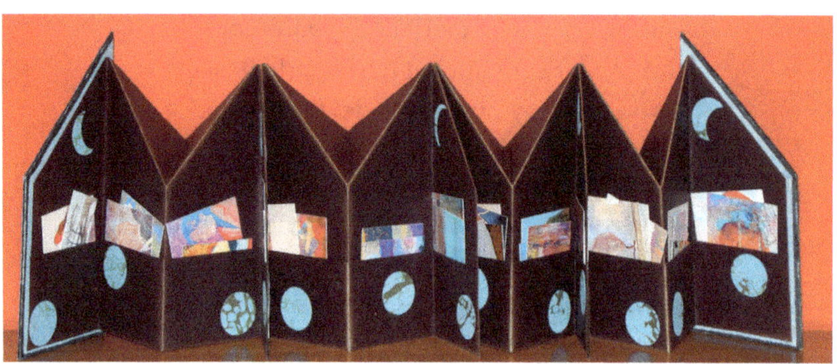

Untitled, 7″x17″

Acknowledgements

Gratitude to someone I know only though his writing—the poet, Rainer Maria Rilke, and his book *Letters to a Young Poet,* the only book I've read multiple times.

In his letter dated October 29, 1903 he writes, "...one slowly learns to recognize the very few Things ... that one can love and something solitary that one can gently take part in." Reading this passage caused me to pick up a paintbrush and become an artist, and Lois Read caused me to start writing poetry. Poetry and art are my "very few Things."

With much gratitude to Frank Simons who lovingly offered to edit my poems.

Acknowledgement by poem:

- Cats Cavorting Crazily, Frank Simons co-author.
- Delicious, inspired by italics from Patricia Engle, Infinite County
- The Path Not Taken, italics a term referring to "two talented individuals working closely together for a common goal."
- An Artist's Story, italics from "Longing" by William Faulkner.
- Seven Circles, block print image by Frank Simons of the International Flag of Planet Earth by Oskar Peenefeldt 2015.
- Earth Day 2023, tiger photograph by Patricia Audet
- Locked in Locked Out, inspired by Patricia Engle, Infinite Country "this country locks you in until it locks you out."
- The Girl, italics Joni Mitchell's The Circle Game
- Our Singing Poet, italics Andy Ross poet guitar player and singer

- Tribute, italics the Bellamy Brothers song: If I Said You Had a Beautiful Body
- Momentum, italics Reiner Marie Rilke, in his book Letters To Young Poet
- Photograph of Dogwood II by Joe Andricosky

www.ingramcontent.com/pod-product-compliance
Lightning Source LLC
LaVergne TN
LVHW010619110826
845149LV00003B/977

* 9 7 8 1 9 6 9 1 2 2 0 6 4 *